Student Edition

STRIVING TOGETHER

what teamwork looks like in the local church

TIM CHRISTOSON

First published in 2013 by Striving Together Publications, a ministry of Lancaster Baptist Church, Lancaster, CA 93535. Striving Together Publications is committed to providing tried, trusted, and proven books that will further equip local churches to carry out the Great Commission. Your comments and suggestions are valued.

Striving Together Publications
4020 E. Lancaster Blvd.
Lancaster, CA 93535
800.201.7748

Cover design by Andrew Hutchens
Layout by Breanna Hawkins
Special thanks to our proofreaders

The author and publication team have put forth every effort to give proper credit to quotes and thoughts that are not original with the author. It is not our intent to claim originality with any quote or thought that could not readily be tied to an original source.

ISBN 978-1-59894-231-6

Printed in the United States of America

Table of Contents

LESSON ONE

Striving in Ministry

Key Verses

1 Corinthians 3:3–15

3 *For ye are yet carnal: for whereas there is among you envying, and strife, and divisions, are ye not carnal, and walk as men?*

4 *For while one saith, I am of Paul; and another, I am of Apollos; are ye not carnal?*

5 *Who then is Paul, and who is Apollos, but ministers by whom ye believed, even as the Lord gave to every man?*

6 *I have planted, Apollos watered; but God gave the increase.*

7 *So then neither is he that planteth any thing, neither he that watereth; but God that giveth the increase.*

8 *Now he that planteth and he that watereth are one: and every man shall receive his own reward according to his own labour.*

9 *For we are labourers together with God: ye are God's husbandry, ye are God's building.*

10 *According to the grace of God which is given unto me, as a wise masterbuilder, I have laid the foundation, and another buildeth thereon. But let every man take heed how he buildeth thereupon.*

11 *For other foundation can no man lay than that is laid, which is Jesus Christ.*

12 *Now if any man build upon this foundation gold, silver, precious stones, wood, hay, stubble;*

13 *Every man's work shall be made manifest: for the day shall declare it, because it shall be revealed by fire; and the fire shall try every man's work of what sort it is.*

14 If any man's work abide which he hath built thereupon, he shall receive a reward.
15 If any man's work shall be burned, he shall suffer loss: but he himself shall be saved; yet so as by fire.

Overview

As members of the local church we must work together as a team to see souls saved, lives changed, and the work of God accomplished.

Introduction

____

____

____

Philippians 1:27

27 Only let your conversation be as it becometh the gospel of Christ: that whether I come and see you, or else be absent, I may hear of your affairs, that ye stand fast in one spirit, with one mind striving together for the faith of the gospel;

I. The Mistake of ____________________ in Ministry (vv. 3–4)

Ephesians 2:19

19 Now therefore ye are no more strangers and foreigners, but fellowcitizens with the saints, and of the household of God;

1 Timothy 5:1–2

1 Rebuke not an elder, but intreat him as a father; and the younger men as brethren;

2 The elder women as mothers; the younger as sisters, with all purity.

A. The ______________________ of their behavior (v. 3)

Matthew 12:34

34 O generation of vipers, how can ye, being evil, speak good things? for out of the abundance of the heart the mouth speaketh.

Numbers 11:1

1 *And when the people complained, it displeased the Lord...*

Proverbs 13:10

10 *Only by pride cometh contention: but with the well advised is wisdom.*

1 Peter 5:5

5 *Likewise, ye younger, submit yourselves unto the elder. Yea, all of you be subject one to another, and be clothed with humility: for God resisteth the proud, and giveth grace to the humble.*

John 17:21

21 *That they all may be one; as thou, Father, art in me, and I in thee, that they also may be one in us: that the world may believe that thou hast sent me.*

B. The ______________________ about their behavior (v. 4)

Ephesians 4:24

24 *And that ye put on the new man, which after God is created in righteousness and true holiness.*

Colossians 3:10

10 *And have put on the new man, which is renewed in knowledge after the image of him that created him:*

Romans 8:7

7 *Because the carnal mind is enmity against God: for it is not subject to the law of God, neither indeed can be.*

II. The Miracle of ______________ in Ministry (vv. 5–10)

A. There was a division of ______________. (vv. 5–8)

ROMANS 12:4–6

4 For as we have many members in one body, and all members have not the same office:
5 So we, being many, are one body in Christ, and every one members one of another.
6 Having then gifts differing according to the grace that is given to us…

MATTHEW 20:28

28 Even as the Son of man came not to be ministered unto, but to minister, and to give his life a ransom for many.

HEBREWS 6:10

10 For God is not unrighteous to forget your work and labour of love, which ye have shewed toward his name, in that ye have ministered to the saints, and do minister.

B. There was a divine ______________. (vv. 9–10)

MATTHEW 28:20

20 …lo, I am with you alway, even unto the end of the world.

JOHN 15:5

5 I am the vine, ye are the branches: He that abideth in me, and I in him, the same bringeth forth much fruit: for without me ye can do nothing.

III. The Materials for ________________ in Ministry (vv. 11–15)

A. The ________________ of our materials (v. 12)

2 Corinthians 4:18

18 While we look not at the things which are seen, but at the things which are not seen: for the things which are seen are temporal; but the things which are not seen are eternal.

Colossians 3:1–2

1 If ye then be risen with Christ, seek those things which are above, where Christ sitteth on the right hand of God.
2 Set your affection on things above, not on things on the earth.

B. The ________________ of our works (v. 13)

2 Corinthians 5:10

10 For we must all appear before the judgment seat of Christ; that every one may receive the things done in his body, according to that he hath done, whether it be good or bad.

Hebrews 4:13

13 Neither is there any creature that is not manifest in his sight: but all things are naked and opened unto the eyes of him with whom we have to do.

C. The ____________ of our judgment (vv. 14–15)

2 TIMOTHY 4:7–8

7 *I have fought a good fight, I have finished my course, I have kept the faith:*

8 *Henceforth there is laid up for me a crown of righteousness, which the Lord, the righteous judge, shall give me at that day: and not to me only, but unto all them also that love his appearing.*

Conclusion

____

____

____

Study Questions

1. According to 1 Corinthians 13:3, what characterized the behavior of the Christians at Corinth?

2. What was the source of their competition?

3. As we seek to serve God in ministry, where should we place our reliance?

4. When will our works for God "be made manifest"?

5. List one action you can take to foster a spirit of teamwork and cooperativeness as you serve the Lord in ministry this week.

6. In what area do you need to rely on God this week?

7. Identify the specific responsibilities God has given you to serve Him in.

8. God has given us resources in addition to our responsibilities. What are some heavenly, eternal materials we should use to build our lives and ministries?

Memory Verse

Philippians 1:27

27 Only let your conversation be as it becometh the gospel of Christ: that whether I come and see you, or else be absent, I may hear of your affairs, that ye stand fast in one spirit, with one mind striving together for the faith of the gospel;

LESSON TWO

Striving at Home

Key Verses

Ephesians 5:31–6:4

31 *For this cause shall a man leave his father and mother, and shall be joined unto his wife, and they two shall be one flesh.*

32 *This is a great mystery: but I speak concerning Christ and the church.*

33 *Nevertheless let every one of you in particular so love his wife even as himself; and the wife see that she reverence her husband.*

6:1 *Children, obey your parents in the Lord: for this is right.*

2 *Honour thy father and mother; (which is the first commandment with promise;)*

3 *That it may be well with thee, and thou mayest live long on the earth.*

4 *And, ye fathers, provoke not your children to wrath: but bring them up in the nurture and admonition of the Lord.*

Overview

Each member of the family must cultivate specific biblical behaviors in order to produce Christ-honoring unity in their home.

Introduction

____

____

____

I. We Must Seek His ________ (5:18–21)

EPHESIANS 5:18–21

18 And be not drunk with wine, wherein is excess; but be filled with the Spirit;
19 Speaking to yourselves in psalms and hymns and spiritual songs, singing and making melody in your heart to the Lord;
20 Giving thanks always for all things unto God and the Father in the name of our Lord Jesus Christ;
21 Submitting yourselves one to another in the fear of God.

A. We will have a ____________________.

1 CORINTHIANS 6:19–20

19 What? know ye not that your body is the temple of the Holy Ghost which is in you, which ye have of God, and ye are not your own?
20 For ye are bought with a price: therefore glorify God in your body, and in your spirit, which are God's.

DEUTERONOMY 31:12–13

12 Gather the people together, men, and women, and children, and thy stranger that is within thy gates, that

they may hear, and that they may learn, and fear the Lord *your God, and observe to do all the words of this law:*
13 *And that their children, which have not known any thing, may hear, and learn to fear the* Lord *your God, as long as ye live in the land whither ye go over Jordan to possess it.*

Train up your child in the way he should go. And walk there yourself once in a while, too! —Author unknown

B. We will have a ________________________.

Philippians 4:4
4 *Rejoice in the Lord alway: and again I say, Rejoice.*

C. We will have a ________________________.

Colossians 3:1–2
1 *If ye then be risen with Christ, seek those things which are above, where Christ sitteth on the right hand of God.*
2 *Set your affection on things above, not on things on the earth.*

1 John 2:15
15 *Love not the world, neither the things that are in the world. If any man love the world, the love of the Father is not in him.*

1 Timothy 6:6–10
6 *But godliness with contentment is great gain.*

7 For we brought nothing into this world, and it is certain we can carry no thing out.
8 And having food and raiment let us be therewith content.
9 But they that will be rich fall into temptation and a snare, and into many foolish and hurtful lusts, which drown men in destruction and perdition.
10 For the love of money is the root of all evil: which while some coveted after, they have erred from the faith, and pierced themselves through with many sorrows.

HEBREWS 13:5
5 Let your conversation be without covetousness; and be content with such things as ye have: for he hath said, I will never leave thee, nor forsake thee.

PHILIPPIANS 4:6
6 Be careful for nothing; but in every thing by prayer and supplication with thanksgiving let your requests be made known unto God.

D. We will have a ______________________________
__________________________.

ROMANS 12:10
10 Be kindly affectioned one to another with brotherly love; in honour preferring one another;

PHILIPPIANS 2:4
4 Look not every man on his own things, but every man also on the things of others.

II. We Must Understand His __________ (5:22–6:4)

A. God has a pattern for __________________ and ______________. (5:22–33)

The husband and wife are equals before God, but equality of worth is not sameness of function. God created male and female different at the very beginning. And God created men as masculine creatures and females as feminine creatures. We are to celebrate the difference, not discriminate against it. A woman is superior to a man at being a woman and a man is superior to a woman at being a man.—Adrian Rogers

Ephesians 5:25–29
25 *Husbands, love your wives, even as Christ also loved the church, and gave himself for it;*
26 *That he might sanctify and cleanse it with the washing of water by the word,*
27 *That he might present it to himself a glorious church, not having spot, or wrinkle, or any such thing; but that it should be holy and without blemish.*
28 *So ought men to love their wives as their own bodies. He that loveth his wife loveth himself.*
29 *For no man ever yet hated his own flesh; but nourisheth and cherisheth it, even as the Lord the church:*

The problem in America is failure in the highest office in the land, that office being husband and father. —Stu Weber

Ephesians 5:22–24

22 Wives, submit yourselves unto your own husbands, as unto the Lord.

23 For the husband is the head of the wife, even as Christ is the head of the church: and he is the saviour of the body.

24 Therefore as the church is subject unto Christ, so let the wives be to their own husbands in every thing.

B. God has a pattern for ________________ and ________________. (6:1–4)

Ephesians 6:4

4 And, ye fathers, provoke not your children to wrath: but bring them up in the nurture and admonition of the Lord.

Proverbs 23:26

26 My son, give me thine heart, and let thine eyes observe my ways.

Ephesians 6:1–3

1 Children, obey your parents in the Lord: for this is right.

2 Honour thy father and mother; (which is the first commandment with promise;)

3 That it may be well with thee, and thou mayest live long on the earth.

Exodus 20:12

12 Honour thy father and thy mother: that thy days may be long upon the land which the Lord thy God giveth thee.

III. We Must Follow His ____________ (5:18–6:4)

A. Follow the principle of ________ devotion.

GENESIS 2:24
24 *Therefore shall a man leave his father and his mother, and shall cleave unto his wife: and they shall be one flesh.*

MATTHEW 19:4–6
4 *And he answered and said unto them, Have ye not read, that he which made them at the beginning made them male and female,*
5 *And said, For this cause shall a man leave father and mother, and shall cleave to his wife: and they twain shall be one flesh?*
6 *Wherefore they are no more twain, but one flesh. What therefore God hath joined together, let not man put asunder.*

Why let a wonderful marriage go down the tubes because of problems? There are no problems too big to solve—just people too small to solve them. People who get divorced and those who are happily married have basically the same kinds of problems. The difference is in loyalty and commitment. Remember, it is not only *love that sustains marriage but also marriage that sustains love.*—ADRIAN ROGERS

B. Follow the principle of ____________ connection.

1 PETER 3:7
7 *Likewise, ye husbands, dwell with them according to knowledge, giving honour unto the wife, as unto the*

weaker vessel, and as being heirs together of the grace of life; that your prayers be not hindered.

C. Follow the principle of _______ compassion.

1 Peter 3:8

8 Finally, be ye all of one mind, having compassion one of another, love as brethren, be pitiful, be courteous:

Ephesians 4:29–32

29 Let no corrupt communication proceed out of your mouth, but that which is good to the use of edifying, that it may minister grace unto the hearers.

30 And grieve not the holy Spirit of God, whereby ye are sealed unto the day of redemption.

31 Let all bitterness, and wrath, and anger, and clamour, and evil speaking, be put away from you, with all malice:

32 And be ye kind one to another, tenderhearted, forgiving one another, even as God for Christ's sake hath forgiven you.

Conclusion

____

____

____

Study Questions

1. What must we seek if we are to experience unity in our homes and family relationships?

2. According to Ephesians 5:19, what is the result of a sanctified life?

3. What type of love should husbands demonstrate to their wives?

4. What type of love should wives demonstrate to their husbands?

5. To whom does God give the primary responsibility of training and nurturing children?

6. List one or two ways you can connect with your spouse or other family members this week.

7. What behavior can you practice this week to produce togetherness in your home?

8. What can you do this week to help cultivate a spirit of contentment in your life and in the lives of your family members?

Memory Verses

EPHESIANS 4:31–32

31 Let all bitterness, and wrath, and anger, and clamour, and evil speaking, be put away from you, with all malice:

32 And be ye kind one to another, tenderhearted, forgiving one another, even as God for Christ's sake hath forgiven you.

Striving for Revival

Key Verses

Acts 19:8–20

8 *And he went into the synagogue, and spake boldly for the space of three months, disputing and persuading the things concerning the kingdom of God.*

9 *But when divers were hardened, and believed not, but spake evil of that way before the multitude, he departed from them, and separated the disciples, disputing daily in the school of one Tyrannus.*

10 *And this continued by the space of two years; so that all they which dwelt in Asia heard the word of the Lord Jesus, both Jews and Greeks.*

11 *And God wrought special miracles by the hands of Paul:*

12 *So that from his body were brought unto the sick handkerchiefs or aprons, and the diseases departed from them, and the evil spirits went out of them.*

13 *Then certain of the vagabond Jews, exorcists, took upon them to call over them which had evil spirits the name of the Lord Jesus, saying, We adjure you by Jesus whom Paul preacheth.*

14 *And there were seven sons of one Sceva, a Jew, and chief of the priests, which did so.*

15 *And the evil spirit answered and said, Jesus I know, and Paul I know; but who are ye?*

16 *And the man in whom the evil spirit was leaped on them, and overcame them, and prevailed against them, so that they fled out of that house naked and wounded.*

17 And this was known to all the Jews and Greeks also dwelling at Ephesus; and fear fell on them all, and the name of the Lord Jesus was magnified.
18 And many that believed came, and confessed, and shewed their deeds.
19 Many of them also which used curious arts brought their books together, and burned them before all men: and they counted the price of them, and found it fifty thousand pieces of silver.
20 So mightily grew the word of God and prevailed.

Overview

When God's people strive together by spreading His truth, experiencing His power, and yielding to His Word, revival is possible!

Introduction

____

____

____

John 10:10

10 *The thief cometh not, but for to steal, and to kill, and to destroy: I am come that they might have life, and that they might have it more abundantly.*

Psalm 85:6

6 *Wilt thou not revive us again: that thy people may rejoice in thee?*

2 Chronicles 7:14

14 *If my people, which are called by my name, shall humble themselves, and pray, and seek my face, and turn from their wicked ways; then will I hear from heaven, and will forgive their sin, and will heal their land.*

I. Revival Occurs When the ____________ of God is ____________ (vv. 8–10)

Acts 17:2

2 *And Paul, as his manner was, went in unto them, and three sabbath days reasoned with them out of the scriptures,*

A. The Apostle gave a message of ____________. (v. 8)

ACTS 4:31

31 And when they had prayed, the place was shaken where they were assembled together; and they were all filled with the Holy Ghost, and they spake the word of God with boldness.

1 PETER 3:15

15 But sanctify the Lord God in your hearts: and be ready always to give an answer to every man that asketh you a reason of the hope that is in you with meekness and fear:

B. The audience had a mixed ______________. (v. 9)

JOHN 6:66

66 From that time many of his disciples went back, and walked no more with him.

C. Asia was miraculously ________________. (v. 10)

LUKE 24:46–47

46 And said unto them, Thus it is written, and thus it behoved Christ to suffer, and to rise from the dead the third day:

47 And that repentance and remission of sins should be preached in his name among all nations, beginning at Jerusalem.

II. Revival Occurs When the __________ of God is ____________ (vv. 11–16)

A. God's power was ________________. (vv. 11–12)

1 Corinthians 13:8–10

8 Charity never faileth: but whether there be prophecies, they shall fail; whether there be tongues, they shall cease; whether there be knowledge, it shall vanish away.
9 For we know in part, and we prophesy in part.
10 But when that which is perfect is come, then that which is in part shall be done away.

Mark 16:19–20

19 So then after the Lord had spoken unto them, he was received up into heaven, and sat on the right hand of God.
20 And they went forth, and preached every where, the Lord working with them, and confirming the word with signs following. Amen.

2 Corinthians 4:5–7

5 For we preach not ourselves, but Christ Jesus the Lord; and ourselves your servants for Jesus' sake.
6 For God, who commanded the light to shine out of darkness, hath shined in our hearts, to give the light of the knowledge of the glory of God in the face of Jesus Christ.
7 But we have this treasure in earthen vessels, that the excellency of the power may be of God, and not of us.

B. God's power was ____________________. (vv. 13–16)

James 2:19

19 *Thou believest that there is one God; thou doest well: the devils also believe, and tremble.*

Zechariah 4:6

6 *Then he answered and spake unto me, saying, This is the word of the Lord unto Zerubbabel, saying, Not by might, nor by power, but by my spirit, saith the Lord of hosts.*

Matthew 23:25–27

25 *Woe unto you, scribes and Pharisees, hypocrites! for ye make clean the outside of the cup and of the platter, but within they are full of extortion and excess.*
26 *Thou blind Pharisee, cleanse first that which is within the cup and platter, that the outside of them may be clean also.*
27 *Woe unto you, scribes and Pharisees, hypocrites! for ye are like unto whited sepulchres, which indeed appear beautiful outward, but are within full of dead men's bones, and of all uncleanness.*

III. Revival Occurs When the __________ of God _______________ (vv. 17–20)

Acts 19:20

20 *So mightily grew the word of God and prevailed.*

Isaiah 55:11

11 *So shall my word be that goeth forth out of my mouth: it shall not return unto me void, but it shall accomplish that*

which I please, and it shall prosper in the thing whereto I sent it.

HEBREWS 4:12

12 *For the word of God is quick, and powerful, and sharper than any twoedged sword, piercing even to the dividing asunder of soul and spirit, and of the joints and marrow, and is a discerner of the thoughts and intents of the heart.*

A. The Saviour was ________________. (v. 17)

PHILIPPIANS 1:20

20 *According to my earnest expectation and my hope, that in nothing I shall be ashamed, but that with all boldness, as always, so now also Christ shall be magnified in my body, whether it be by life, or by death.*

You cannot find a sermon in the New Testament that does not center on the person and work of Jesus Christ. The apostles were not interested in building their own reputations. They desired to magnify the name of Jesus, and they ensured that the miracles and great works they performed brought honor and glory to the Lord, not themselves.—PAUL CHAPPELL

B. Souls were ______________. (v. 18)

JOHN 4:39

39 *And many of the Samaritans of that city believed on him for the saying of the woman, which testified, He told me all that ever I did.*

John 12:32
32 And I, if I be lifted up from the earth, will draw all men unto me.

Acts 4:4
4 Howbeit many of them which heard the word believed; and the number of the men was about five thousand.

Acts 8:5–6
5 Then Philip went down to the city of Samaria, and preached Christ unto them.
6 And the people with one accord gave heed unto those things which Philip spake, hearing and seeing the miracles which he did.

Acts 9:42
42 And it was known throughout all Joppa; and many believed in the Lord.

Acts 17:12
12 Therefore many of them believed; also of honourable women which were Greeks, and of men, not a few.

I can give you a prescription that will bring a revival to any church or community or any city on earth. The prescription is as follows: First, let a few Christians (they need not be many) get thoroughly right with God themselves. This is the prime essential. If this is not done, the rest that I am to say will come to nothing. Second, let them bind themselves together to pray for a revival until God opens the heavens and comes down. Third, let them put themselves at the disposal of God for Him to use as He sees fit in winning others to Christ. That is all! This is sure to bring a revival to any church or community.—R. A. Torrey

C. The saved were ____________________. (v. 19)

2 CORINTHIANS 5:17

17 Therefore if any man be in Christ, he is a new creature: old things are passed away; behold, all things are become new.

EPHESIANS 5:8

8 For ye were sometimes darkness, but now are ye light in the Lord: walk as children of light:

1 THESSALONIANS 1:9

9 For they themselves shew of us what manner of entering in we had unto you, and how ye turned to God from idols to serve the living and true God;

Conclusion

____

____

____

Study Questions

1. According to our text, when does revival occur?

2. How did the audience respond to Paul's preaching, and what can this teach us about our own witnessing efforts?

3. Name one indication that God's Word is prevailing.

4. In verses 13–16, who tried to copy Paul's miracles?

5. Paul shared his message with boldness and preparation. In what ways could you develop these qualities as you share your faith?

6. Transformation involves turning to God from that which would keep us away from Him. What habits, attitudes, or possessions do you need to forsake in order to experience personal revival?

7. Write out 2 Corinthians 5:17.

8. In what areas do you desire to see God's power manifested in your own life? Take a moment to pray for His power and presence as you are faced with these situations.

Memory Verse

2 Chronicles 7:14

14 If my people, which are called by my name, shall humble themselves, and pray, and seek my face, and turn from their wicked ways; then will I hear from heaven, and will forgive their sin, and will heal their land.

LESSON FOUR

Striving in Relationships

Key Verses

Romans 12:9–21

9 *Let love be without dissimulation. Abhor that which is evil; cleave to that which is good.*

10 *Be kindly affectioned one to another with brotherly love; in honour preferring one another;*

11 *Not slothful in business; fervent in spirit; serving the Lord;*

12 *Rejoicing in hope; patient in tribulation; continuing instant in prayer;*

13 *Distributing to the necessity of saints; given to hospitality.*

14 *Bless them which persecute you: bless, and curse not.*

15 *Rejoice with them that do rejoice, and weep with them that weep.*

16 *Be of the same mind one toward another. Mind not high things, but condescend to men of low estate. Be not wise in your own conceits.*

17 *Recompense to no man evil for evil. Provide things honest in the sight of all men.*

18 *If it be possible, as much as lieth in you, live peaceably with all men.*

19 *Dearly beloved, avenge not yourselves, but rather give place unto wrath: for it is written, Vengeance is mine; I will repay, saith the Lord.*

20 *Therefore if thine enemy hunger, feed him; if he thirst, give him drink: for in so doing thou shalt heap coals of fire on his head.*

21 *Be not overcome of evil, but overcome evil with good.*

Overview

If we will follow the clear and proven instructions in God's Word, we can experience His blessing in our relationships.

Introduction

____

____

____

I. Possessing the Right ______________ (vv. 9–12)

A. We should possess ____________. (vv. 9–10)

Love is the circulatory system of the spiritual body, which enables all the members to function in a healthy, harmonious way.—Warren W. Wiersbe

1 Peter 1:22
22 *Seeing ye have purified your souls in obeying the truth through the Spirit unto unfeigned love of the brethren, see that ye love one another with a pure heart fervently:*

1 John 3:18
18 *My little children, let us not love in word, neither in tongue; but in deed and in truth.*

B. We should possess ________________. (v. 9b)

Romans 16:19
19 *...I would have you wise unto that which is good, and simple concerning evil.*

C. We should possess ________________. (v. 11)

PROVERBS 13:4

4 *The soul of the sluggard desireth, and hath nothing: but the soul of the diligent shall be made fat.*

D. We should possess ________________. (v. 12)

1 PETER 5:7

7 *Casting all your care upon him; for he careth for you.*

2 THESSALONIANS 1:4

4 *So that we ourselves glory in you in the churches of God for your patience and faith in all your persecutions and tribulations that ye endure:*

II. Practicing the Right ________________ (vv. 13–16)

A. We should practice ________________. (v. 13a)

1 JOHN 3:17

17 *But whoso hath this world's good, and seeth his brother have need, and shutteth up his bowels of compassion from him, how dwelleth the love of God in him?*

B. We should practice ________________. (v. 13b)

1 PETER 4:9

9 *Use hospitality one to another without grudging.*

C. We should practice ______________. (v. 15)

1 PETER 3:8
8 Finally, be ye all of one mind, having compassion one of another, love as brethren, be pitiful, be courteous:

D. We should practice ______________. (v. 16)

PHILIPPIANS 2:7–8
7 But made himself of no reputation, and took upon him the form of a servant, and was made in the likeness of men:
8 And being found in fashion as a man, he humbled himself, and became obedient unto death, even the death of the cross.

1 PETER 5:5–6
5 Likewise, ye younger, submit yourselves unto the elder. Yea, all of you be subject one to another, and be clothed with humility: for God resisteth the proud, and giveth grace to the humble.
6 Humble yourselves therefore under the mighty hand of God, that he may exalt you in due time:

PROVERBS 13:10
10 Only by pride cometh contention…

III. Providing the Right ______________ (vv. 14, 17–21)

A. We should provide ________________. (vv. 14, 17a, 19, 20)

The Christian must not play God and try to avenge himself. Returning evil for evil, or good for good, is the way most people live. But the Christian must live on a higher level and return good for evil. Of course, this requires *love*, because our first inclination is to fight back. It also requires *faith*, believing that God can work and accomplish His will in our lives and in the lives of those who hurt us. These words are easy to read but difficult to practice. Will they take advantage of us? Will they hate us more? Only the Lord knows. Our task is not to protect ourselves but to obey the Lord and leave the results with Him.
—Warren W. Wiersbe

Matthew 5:44, 46–47

44 *But I say unto you, Love your enemies, bless them that curse you, do good to them that hate you, and pray for them which despitefully use you, and persecute you;*
46 *For if ye love them which love you, what reward have ye? do not even the publicans the same?*
47 *And if ye salute your brethren only, what do ye more than others? do not even the publicans so?*

B. *We should provide _______________.* *(v. 17b)*

1 Peter 2:12

12 *Having your conversation honest among the Gentiles: that, whereas they speak against you as evildoers, they may by your good works, which they shall behold, glorify God in the day of visitation.*

C. We should provide ________________. (v. 18)

MATTHEW 5:9
9 *Blessed are the peacemakers…*

1 PETER 3:11
11 *Let him eschew evil, and do good; let him seek peace, and ensue it.*

ROMANS 14:19
19 *Let us therefore follow after the things which make for peace, and things wherewith one may edify another.*

D. We should provide ________________. (v. 21)

GALATIANS 5:22–23
22 *But the fruit of the Spirit is love, joy, peace, longsuffering, gentleness, goodness, faith,*
23 *Meekness, temperance: against such there is no law.*

1 PETER 2:19–23
19 *For this is thankworthy, if a man for conscience toward God endure grief, suffering wrongfully.*
20 *For what glory is it, if, when ye be buffeted for your faults, ye shall take it patiently? but if, when ye do well, and suffer for it, ye take it patiently, this is acceptable with God.*
21 *For even hereunto were ye called: because Christ also suffered for us, leaving us an example, that ye should follow his steps:*
22 *Who did no sin, neither was guile found in his mouth:*

23 Who, when he was reviled, reviled not again; when he suffered, he threatened not; but committed himself to him that judgeth righteously:

Conclusion

____

____

____

Study Questions

1. What character traits should we seek to develop if we want to strengthen our relationships?

2. Who is our greatest example in humility?

3. What words should define our response to people who might bother or annoy us?

4. Write out 1 Peter 3:8.

5. How can you demonstrate biblical hospitality this week?

6. Consider your instinctive responses in the context of your relationships. If they can't be described by the adjectives given in the lesson, what specific steps can you take to improve?

7. How can you go the extra mile to prevent frustration and avoid conflict in your relationships?

8. Identify a specific relationship that is struggling right now. What biblical instructions do you need to follow for that relationship?

Memory Verses

Romans 12:9–10

9 *Let love be without dissimulation. Abhor that which is evil; cleave to that which is good.*

10 *Be kindly affectioned one to another with brotherly love; in honour preferring one another;*

LESSON FIVE

Striving in Prayer

Key Verses

ROMANS 15:23–32

23 *But now having no more place in these parts, and having a great desire these many years to come unto you;*

24 *Whensoever I take my journey into Spain, I will come to you: for I trust to see you in my journey, and to be brought on my way thitherward by you, if first I be somewhat filled with your company.*

25 *But now I go unto Jerusalem to minister unto the saints.*

26 *For it hath pleased them of Macedonia and Achaia to make a certain contribution for the poor saints which are at Jerusalem.*

27 *It hath pleased them verily; and their debtors they are. For if the Gentiles have been made partakers of their spiritual things, their duty is also to minister unto them in carnal things.*

28 *When therefore I have performed this, and have sealed to them this fruit, I will come by you into Spain.*

29 *And I am sure that, when I come unto you, I shall come in the fulness of the blessing of the gospel of Christ.*

30 *Now I beseech you, brethren, for the Lord Jesus Christ's sake, and for the love of the Spirit, that ye strive together with me in your prayers to God for me;*

31 *That I may be delivered from them that do not believe in Judaea; and that my service which I have for Jerusalem may be accepted of the saints;*

32 *That I may come unto you with joy by the will of God, and may with you be refreshed.*

Overview

God's people are called to strive together in prayer for one another, for the man of God, and for the advancement of God's work in this world.

Introduction

____

____

____

Hebrews 4:16

16 Let us therefore come boldly unto the throne of grace, that we may obtain mercy, and find grace to help in time of need.

Acts 4:31–33

31 And when they had prayed, the place was shaken where they were assembled together; and they were all filled with the Holy Ghost, and they spake the word of God with boldness.
32 And the multitude of them that believed were of one heart and of one soul: neither said any of them that ought of the things which he possessed was his own; but they had all things common.
33 And with great power gave the apostles witness of the resurrection of the Lord Jesus: and great grace was upon them all.

James 5:15

15 And the prayer of faith shall save the sick, and the Lord shall raise him up; and if he have committed sins, they shall be forgiven him.

I. The Strategic ______________ of Paul (vv. 23–28)

A. Paul planned to ____________ the converts in Rome. (v. 23)

ROMANS 1:9–13

9 For God is my witness, whom I serve with my spirit in the gospel of his Son, that without ceasing I make mention of you always in my prayers;

10 Making request, if by any means now at length I might have a prosperous journey by the will of God to come unto you.

11 For I long to see you, that I may impart unto you some spiritual gift, to the end ye may be established;

12 That is, that I may be comforted together with you by the mutual faith both of you and me.

13 Now I would not have you ignorant, brethren, that oftentimes I purposed to come unto you, (but was let hitherto,) that I might have some fruit among you also, even as among other Gentiles.

B. Paul planned to ______________________ the citizens of Spain. (v. 24)

ROMANS 15:20

20 Yea, so have I strived to preach the gospel, not where Christ was named, lest I should build upon another man's foundation:

C. Paul planned to ______________________ the Christians in Jerusalem. (vv. 25–28)

ROMANS 1:14

14 I am debtor both to the Greeks, and to the Barbarians; both to the wise, and to the unwise.

2 Corinthians 8:1–4

1 Moreover, brethren, we do you to wit of the grace of God bestowed on the churches of Macedonia;

2 How that in a great trial of affliction the abundance of their joy and their deep poverty abounded unto the riches of their liberality.

3 For to their power, I bear record, yea, and beyond their power they were willing of themselves;

4 Praying us with much intreaty that we would receive the gift, and take upon us the fellowship of the ministering to the saints.

II. The Striving ________________ in Prayer (vv. 29–30)

A. Paul had confidence in ____________ prayer. (v. 29)

1 John 5:14–15

14 And this is the confidence that we have in him, that, if we ask any thing according to his will, he heareth us:

15 And if we know that he hear us, whatsoever we ask, we know that we have the petitions that we desired of him.

One of the terrible marks of the diseased state of Christian life these days is that there are so many who are content without the distinct experience of answer to prayer. They pray daily, they ask many things, and they trust that some of them will be heard. But they know little of direct, definite, answer to prayer as the rule of daily life.—Andrew Murray

B. Paul had a concern for __________________ in prayer. (v. 30)

Luke 11:8

8 I say unto you, Though he will not rise and give him, because he is his friend, yet because of his importunity he will rise and give him as many as he needeth.

The expression *striving together* suggests an athlete giving his best in the contest. Our praying must not be a casual experience that has no heart or earnestness. We should put as much fervor into our praying as a wrestler does into his wrestling.—Warren W. Wiersbe

Colossians 4:12

12 Epaphras, who is one of you, a servant of Christ, saluteth you, always labouring fervently for you in prayers, that ye may stand perfect and complete in all the will of God.

C. Paul had a concept of __________________ in prayer. (v. 30)

It is part of the genius of Christianity that any believer can become a warrior in the battle at any time and in any place and make his influence count to the ends of the earth and high in heavenly places, simply by engaging in prayer.—John Phillips

Matthew 18:18–20

18 Verily I say unto you, Whatsoever ye shall bind on earth shall be bound in heaven: and whatsoever ye shall loose on earth shall be loosed in heaven.

19 Again I say unto you, That if two of you shall agree on earth as touching any thing that they shall ask, it shall be done for them of my Father which is in heaven.
20 For where two or three are gathered together in my name, there am I in the midst of them.

III. The Specific ________________ Plea (vv. 31–32)

A. Paul asked for ________________ from the ________________. (v. 31a)

2 Corinthians 11:23–27
23 Are they ministers of Christ? (I speak as a fool) I am more; in labours more abundant, in stripes above measure, in prisons more frequent, in deaths oft.
24 Of the Jews five times received I forty stripes save one.
25 Thrice was I beaten with rods, once was I stoned, thrice I suffered shipwreck, a night and a day I have been in the deep;
26 In journeyings often, in perils of waters, in perils of robbers, in perils by mine own countrymen, in perils by the heathen, in perils in the city, in perils in the wilderness, in perils in the sea, in perils among false brethren;
27 In weariness and painfulness, in watchings often, in hunger and thirst, in fastings often, in cold and nakedness.

2 Timothy 4:16–18
16 At my first answer no man stood with me, but all men forsook me: I pray God that it may not be laid to their charge.

17 Notwithstanding the Lord stood with me, and strengthened me; that by me the preaching might be fully known, and that all the Gentiles might hear: and I was delivered out of the mouth of the lion.
18 And the Lord shall deliver me from every evil work, and will preserve me unto his heavenly kingdom: to whom be glory for ever and ever. Amen.

B. Paul asked for ________________________ in ________________________. (v. 31b)

Colossians 4:3
3 Withal praying also for us, that God would open unto us a door of utterance, to speak the mystery of Christ, for which I am also in bonds:

2 Thessalonians 3:1
1 Finally, brethren, pray for us, that the word of the Lord may have free course, and be glorified, even as it is with you:

C. Paul asked for __________________________ ________________________. (v. 32)

James 4:13–15
13 Go to now, ye that say, To day or to morrow we will go into such a city, and continue there a year, and buy and sell, and get gain:
14 Whereas ye know not what shall be on the morrow. For what is your life? It is even a vapour, that appeareth for a little time, and then vanisheth away.
15 For that ye ought to say, If the Lord will, we shall live, and do this, or that.

Acts 24:14–15

14 *Where we found brethren, and were desired to tarry with them seven days: and so we went toward Rome.*

15 *And from thence, when the brethren heard of us, they came to meet us as far as Appii forum, and The three taverns: whom when Paul saw, he thanked God, and took courage.*

Conclusion

____

____

____

Study Questions

1. What was Paul's desire for the citizens in Spain?

2. What was one main way Paul wanted to encourage the poverty-stricken Christians in Jerusalem?

3. What three specific prayer requests did Paul make in verses 31–32 that we can also pray for ourselves?

4. Write out 1 John 5:14.

5. Paul had a strong desire to see the world come to Christ. List the names of those you are specifically praying for to accept Christ as their Saviour.

6. In what area of your life do you need to demonstrate confidence in God to answer your prayer?

7. In what area of your life do you need to demonstrate surrender to God's providential guidance in how He answers your prayer?

8. As a small group or church, what are you currently striving together for in prayer?

Memory Verses

Matthew 18:19–20

19 Again I say unto you, That if two of you shall agree on earth as touching any thing that they shall ask, it shall be done for them of my Father which is in heaven.

20 For where two or three are gathered together in my name, there am I in the midst of them.

LESSON SIX

Striving in Unity

Key Verses

Acts 2:41–47

41 Then they that gladly received his word were baptized: and the same day there were added unto them about three thousand souls.

42 And they continued stedfastly in the apostles' doctrine and fellowship, and in breaking of bread, and in prayers.

43 And fear came upon every soul: and many wonders and signs were done by the apostles.

44 And all that believed were together, and had all things common;

45 And sold their possessions and goods, and parted them to all men, as every man had need.

46 And they, continuing daily with one accord in the temple, and breaking bread from house to house, did eat their meat with gladness and singleness of heart,

47 Praising God, and having favour with all the people. And the Lord added to the church daily such as should be saved.

Overview

God's plan is for His people to work in harmony, to follow His lead, and to accomplish His work in this world. Since unity doesn't occur naturally, this requires intentional efforts along the way—efforts modeled well by the early church.

Introduction

____

____

____

ROMANS 15:5–6

5 *Now the God of patience and consolation grant you to be likeminded one toward another according to Christ Jesus:*

6 *That ye may with one mind and one mouth glorify God, even the Father of our Lord Jesus Christ.*

I. Spiritual ____________________ (vv. 41–42)

A. The believers started ____________. (v. 41)

JAMES 1:21

21 *…receive with meekness the engrafted word, which is able to save your souls.*

1 PETER 1:23

23 *Being born again, not of corruptible seed, but of incorruptible, by the word of God, which liveth and abideth for ever.*

MATTHEW 28:19

19 *Go ye therefore, and teach all nations, baptizing them in the name of the Father, and of the Son, and of the Holy Ghost:"*

Ephesians 2:19

19 Now therefore ye are no more strangers and foreigners, but fellowcitizens with the saints, and of the household of God;

B. The believers were ________________. (v. 42)

John 8:31

31 Then said Jesus to those Jews which believed on him, If ye continue in my word, then are ye my disciples indeed;

1 Timothy 4:13

13 Till I come, give attendance to reading, to exhortation, to doctrine.

Romans 12:10

10 Be kindly affectioned one to another with brotherly love; in honour preferring one another;

1 Corinthians 11:23–28

23 For I have received of the Lord that which also I delivered unto you, That the Lord Jesus the same night in which he was betrayed took bread:
24 And when he had given thanks, he brake it, and said, Take, eat: this is my body, which is broken for you: this do in remembrance of me.
25 After the same manner also he took the cup, when he had supped, saying, This cup is the new testament in my blood: this do ye, as oft as ye drink it, in remembrance of me.
26 For as often as ye eat this bread, and drink this cup, ye do shew the Lord's death till he come.

27 Wherefore whosoever shall eat this bread, and drink this cup of the Lord, unworthily, shall be guilty of the body and blood of the Lord.
28 But let a man examine himself, and so let him eat of that bread, and drink of that cup.

PHILIPPIANS 4:6
6 Be careful for nothing; but in every thing by prayer and supplication with thanksgiving let your requests be made known unto God.

II. Sacrificial ______________ (vv. 44–45)

A. Their ____________________ was spiritual. (v. 44)

ACTS 4:32
32 And the multitude of them that believed were of one heart and of one soul: neither said any of them that ought of the things which he possessed was his own; but they had all things common.

B. Their ____________________ were sold. (v. 45a)

2 CORINTHIANS 8:9
9 For ye know the grace of our Lord Jesus Christ, that, though he was rich, yet for your sakes he became poor, that ye through his poverty might be rich.

ACTS 4:34–37
34 Neither was there any among them that lacked: for as many as were possessors of lands or houses sold them, and brought the prices of the things that were sold,

35 And laid them down at the apostles' feet: and distribution was made unto every man according as he had need.
36 And Joses, who by the apostles was surnamed Barnabas, (which is, being interpreted, The son of consolation,) a Levite, and of the country of Cyprus,
37 Having land, sold it, and brought the money, and laid it at the apostles' feet.

C. Their ________________ were shared. (v. 45b)

1 CHRONICLES 29:14
14 But who am I, and what is my people, that we should be able to offer so willingly after this sort? for all things come of thee, and of thine own have we given thee.

III. Sincere ________________ (vv. 46–47)

A. They ________________ frequently. (v. 46)

HEBREWS 10:24–25
24 And let us consider one another to provoke unto love and to good works:
25 Not forsaking the assembling of ourselves together, as the manner of some is; but exhorting one another: and so much the more, as ye see the day approaching.

B. They ________________ the Father. (v. 47a)

1 PETER 4:11
11 If any man speak, let him speak as the oracles of God; if any man minister, let him do it as of the ability

which God giveth: that God in all things may be glorified through Jesus Christ, to whom be praise and dominion for ever and ever. Amen.

C. They ____________________ favor. (v. 47b)

[Gladness] was the keynote of the church. The people were happy. No wonder their numbers grew. There was no complaining, no criticizing, no envy, no strife. The fruit of the Spirit was everywhere—'love, joy, peace, longsuffering, gentleness, goodness, faith, meekness, temperance' (Galatians 5:22–23). What an attractive company of people it was—a company of people praising God!—John Phillips

Matthew 5:16
16 Let your light so shine before men, that they may see your good works, and glorify your Father which is in heaven.

Conclusion

____

____

____

Philippians 2:4
4 Look not every man on his own things, but every man also on the things of others.

Study Questions

1. What three main factors contributed to the Christians' unity in Acts 2?

2. According to Acts 2:41, what three events mark the start of a believer's spiritual growth?

3. Define sacrificial giving.

4. How do we know the Christians in Acts possessed sincere gladness?

5. Describe your perspective on sacrificial giving. Does it match the perspective shared by the Christians in Acts 4:32?

6. Are you currently enjoying spiritual growth? What steps can you take to continue your growth journey?

7. What can you do to specifically and sacrificially meet the need of another?

8. Are your closest relationships centered around Christ and His followers? How can you cultivate these relationships?

Memory Verses

Hebrews 10:24–25

24 And let us consider one another to provoke unto love and to good works:

25 Not forsaking the assembling of ourselves together, as the manner of some is; but exhorting one another: and so much the more, as ye see the day approaching.

Striving in Forgiveness

Key Verses

MATTHEW 18:23–35

23 *Therefore is the kingdom of heaven likened unto a certain king, which would take account of his servants.*
24 *And when he had begun to reckon, one was brought unto him, which owed him ten thousand talents.*
25 *But forasmuch as he had not to pay, his lord commanded him to be sold, and his wife, and children, and all that he had, and payment to be made.*
26 *The servant therefore fell down, and worshipped him, saying, Lord, have patience with me, and I will pay thee all.*
27 *Then the lord of that servant was moved with compassion, and loosed him, and forgave him the debt.*
28 *But the same servant went out, and found one of his fellowservants, which owed him an hundred pence: and he laid hands on him, and took him by the throat, saying, Pay me that thou owest.*
29 *And his fellowservant fell down at his feet, and besought him, saying, Have patience with me, and I will pay thee all.*
30 *And he would not: but went and cast him into prison, till he should pay the debt.*
31 *So when his fellowservants saw what was done, they were very sorry, and came and told unto their lord all that was done.*
32 *Then his lord, after that he had called him, said unto him, O thou wicked servant, I forgave thee all that debt, because thou desiredst me:*
33 *Shouldest not thou also have had compassion on thy fellowservant, even as I had pity on thee?*

34 And his lord was wroth, and delivered him to the tormentors, till he should pay all that was due unto him.
35 So likewise shall my heavenly Father do also unto you, if ye from your hearts forgive not every one his brother their trespasses.

Overview

One of the most important lessons Jesus would leave with His disciples was the lesson of forgiveness. It's the one act we are *all* required to perform as Christians. Not all of Christ's followers will preach a sermon, travel as a missionary, or suffer persecution at the hands of human government. But *all* Christians seeking to strive together for Christ are given the opportunity to extend forgiveness.

Introduction

____

____

____

MATTHEW 18:21
21 Then came Peter to him, and said, Lord, how oft shall my brother sin against me, and I forgive him? till seven times?

I. The ____________________ in Forgiveness (vv. 23–30)

A. There is an ____________________. (vv. 24, 28)

JOHN 16:33
33 These things I have spoken unto you, that in me ye might have peace. In the world ye shall have tribulation: but be of good cheer; I have overcome the world.

MATTHEW 18:15–16
15 Moreover if thy brother shall trespass against thee, go and tell him his fault between thee and him alone: if he shall hear thee, thou hast gained thy brother.
16 But if he will not hear thee, then take with thee one or two more, that in the mouth of two or three witnesses every word may be established.

B. There is the ____________________________.
(vv. 26, 29)

MATTHEW 5:23–24
23 Therefore if thou bring thy gift to the altar, and there rememberest that thy brother hath ought against thee;
24 Leave there thy gift before the altar, and go thy way; first be reconciled to thy brother, and then come and offer thy gift.

C. There is an ____________________________.
(vv. 23, 27, 31)

EPHESIANS 4:32
32 And be ye kind one to another, tenderhearted, forgiving one another, even as God for Christ's sake hath forgiven you.

II. The ________________________ of Forgiveness (vv. 31–33)

A. Forgiveness is preceded by
____________________________.

LUKE 17:3
3 Take heed to yourselves: If thy brother trespass against thee, rebuke him; and if he repent, forgive him.

B. Forgiveness sometimes requires
____________________________.

Luke 17:4
4 *And if he trespass against thee seven times in a day, and seven times in a day turn again to thee, saying, I repent; thou shalt forgive him.*

C. Forgiveness is _____________________.

Hebrews 10:17
17 *And their sins and iniquities will I remember no more.*

D. Forgiveness is _____________________.

Colossians 3:13
13 *Forbearing one another, and forgiving one another, if any man have a quarrel against any: even as Christ forgave you, so also do ye.*

E. Forgiveness prohibits _______________.

1 Peter 2:23
23 *Who, when he was reviled, reviled not again; when he suffered, he threatened not; but committed himself to him that judgeth righteously:*

F. Forgiveness prevents _______________.

Hebrews 12:15
15 *Looking diligently lest any man fail of the grace of God; lest any root of bitterness springing up trouble you, and thereby many be defiled;*

Bitterness is the poison we swallow in our effort to harm the one who wronged us.—Author unknown

III. The ________________ of Forgiveness (vv. 33–35)

A. ________________ is a priority. (v. 33)

Psalm 145:8
8 *The Lord is gracious, and full of compassion; slow to anger, and of great mercy.*

Psalm 86:5
5 *For thou, Lord, art good, and ready to forgive; and plenteous in mercy unto all them that call upon thee.*

Matthew 9:36
36 *But when he saw the multitudes, he was moved with compassion on them, because they fainted, and were scattered abroad, as sheep having no shepherd.*

B. ________________ is a priority. (vv. 34–35)

Matthew 6:14–15
14 *For if ye forgive men their trespasses, your heavenly Father will also forgive you:*
15 *But if ye forgive not men their trespasses, neither will your Father forgive your trespasses.*

Conclusion

____

____

____

Study Questions

1. When dealing with forgiveness, what is the responsibility of the person who has been offended?

2. What is the responsibility of the person who has caused the offense?

3. Who is the main character in the participants of forgiveness and how does He make a difference?

4. In an effort to strive together with other believers, what principle of forgiveness (listed under point 2) is most needed for implementation in your own life?

5. What phrase is used to describe the extent of God's compassion and forgiveness in Psalm 86:5?

6. According to Colossians 3:13, what is our greatest motivator in forgiveness?

7. Is forgiveness a choice that is left to us to make or is it a command given by God?

8. Take inventory of your relationships. Do any require forgiveness or repentance? List any specific steps that need to be taken to restore a spirit of unity as you strive together in God-given relationships.

Memory Verse

Ephesians 4:32
32 *And be ye kind one to another, tenderhearted, forgiving one another, even as God for Christ's sake hath forgiven you.*

LESSON EIGHT

Striving with Confidence in God

Text

Philippians 4:10–20

10 *But I rejoiced in the Lord greatly, that now at the last your care of me hath flourished again; wherein ye were also careful, but ye lacked opportunity.*

11 *Not that I speak in respect of want: for I have learned, in whatsoever state I am, therewith to be content.*

12 *I know both how to be abased, and I know how to abound: every where and in all things I am instructed both to be full and to be hungry, both to abound and to suffer need.*

13 *I can do all things through Christ which strengtheneth me.*

14 *Notwithstanding ye have well done, that ye did communicate with my affliction.*

15 *Now ye Philippians know also, that in the beginning of the gospel, when I departed from Macedonia, no church communicated with me as concerning giving and receiving, but ye only.*

16 *For even in Thessalonica ye sent once and again unto my necessity.*

17 *Not because I desire a gift: but I desire fruit that may abound to your account.*

18 *But I have all, and abound: I am full, having received of Epaphroditus the things which were sent from you, an odour of a sweet smell, a sacrifice acceptable, wellpleasing to God.*

19 *But my God shall supply all your need according to his riches in glory by Christ Jesus.*

20 *Now unto God and our Father be glory for ever and ever. Amen.*

Overview

When we are called on to exercise generosity or sacrifice as we strive together, we must first possess a confidence in God's ability to supply our needs.

Introduction

____

____

____

Romans 3:23
23 *For all have sinned, and come short of the glory of God;*

Hebrews 11:6
6 *But without faith it is impossible to please him: for he that cometh to God must believe that he is, and that he is a rewarder of them that diligently seek him.*

I. The ____________________ of Placing Confidence in God (vv. 10–13)

A. Paul's confidence produced ____________. (v. 10)

Philippians 4:4
4 *Rejoice in the Lord alway: and again I say, Rejoice.*

Romans 8:28
28 *And we know that all things work together for good to them that love God, to them who are the called according to his purpose.*

Philippians 1:12
12 *But I would ye should understand, brethren, that the things which happened unto me have fallen out rather unto the furtherance of the gospel;*

B. Paul's confidence produced ________________________. (vv. 11–12)

1 TIMOTHY 6:6–10

6 But godliness with contentment is great gain.
7 For we brought nothing into this world, and it is certain we can carry nothing out.
8 And having food and raiment let us be therewith content.
9 But they that will be rich fall into temptation and a snare, and into many foolish and hurtful lusts, which drown men in destruction and perdition.
10 For the love of money is the root of all evil: which while some coveted after, they have erred from the faith, and pierced themselves through with many sorrows.

C. Paul's confidence produced ______________. (v. 13)

All of nature depends on hidden resources. The great trees send their roots down into the earth to draw up water and minerals. Rivers have their sources in the snow-capped mountains. The most important part of a tree is the part you cannot see, the root system; and the most important part of the Christian's life is the part that only God sees. Unless we draw upon the deep resources of God by faith, we fail against the pressures of life. Paul depended on the power of Christ at work in his life. 'I can—through Christ!' was Paul's motto, and it can be our motto too.—WARREN W. WIERSBE

MARK 10:27

27 And Jesus looking upon them saith, With men it is impossible, but not with God: for with God all things are possible.

II. The ________________ who Practiced Confidence in God (vv. 14–18)

A. They ____________________________ and they gave. (vv. 10, 14–16)

2 Corinthians 8:1–4

1 Moreover, brethren, we do you to wit of the grace of God bestowed on the churches of Macedonia;
2 How that in a great trial of affliction the abundance of their joy and their deep poverty abounded unto the riches of their liberality.
3 For to their power, I bear record, yea, and beyond their power they were willing of themselves;
4 Praying us with much intreaty that we would receive the gift, and take upon us the fellowship of the ministering to the saints.

B. They ____________________________ when they gave. (v. 17)

Galatians 6:7–9

7 Be not deceived; God is not mocked: for whatsoever a man soweth, that shall he also reap.
8 For he that soweth to his flesh shall of the flesh reap corruption; but he that soweth to the Spirit shall of the Spirit reap life everlasting.
9 And let us not be weary in well doing: for in due season we shall reap, if we faint not.

Giving is not a debt we owe; it's a seed we sow. —Author unknown

C. They practiced ____________________ as they gave. (vv. 15–16, 18)

1 PETER 2:5

5 Ye also, as lively stones, are built up a spiritual house, an holy priesthood, to offer up spiritual sacrifices, acceptable to God by Jesus Christ.

III. The ________________ that Provides Confidence in God (vv. 19–20)

A. Consider the ____________________ of God's promise. (v. 19a)

LUKE 6:38

38 Give, and it shall be given unto you; good measure, pressed down, and shaken together, and running over, shall men give into your bosom. For with the same measure that ye mete withal it shall be measured to you again.

PSALM 37:25

25 I have been young, and now am old; yet have I not seen the righteous forsaken, nor his seed begging bread.

When God's work is done in God's way for God's glory, it will not lack for God's supply.—HUDSON TAYLOR

B. Consider the ____________________ of God's promise. (v. 19b)

PSALM 50:10–12

10 For every beast of the forest is mine, and the cattle upon a thousand hills.

11 I know all the fowls of the mountains: and the wild beasts of the field are mine.
12 If I were hungry, I would not tell thee: for the world is mine, and the fulness thereof.

C. Consider the ____________________ of God's promise. (v. 20)

1 KINGS 18:36–39
36 And it came to pass at the time of the offering of the evening sacrifice, that Elijah the prophet came near, and said, LORD God of Abraham, Isaac, and of Israel, let it be known this day that thou art God in Israel, and that I am thy servant, and that I have done all these things at thy word.
37 Hear me, O LORD, hear me, that this people may know that thou art the LORD God, and that thou hast turned their heart back again.
38 Then the fire of the LORD fell, and consumed the burnt sacrifice, and the wood, and the stones, and the dust, and licked up the water that was in the trench.
39 And when all the people saw it, they fell on their faces: and they said, The LORD, he is the God; the LORD, he is the God.

Conclusion

____

____

____

Study Questions

1. It is easy to place our confidence in many things. List some common examples.

2. Where should our complete trust and confidence be found?

3. What three characteristics did Paul's confidence in God produce?

4. In Philippians 4:10 (and as a recurring theme in book of Philippians), what specific characteristic do we see that is a result of placing confidence in God?

5. How did the Christians at Philippi practice, or demonstrate, their confidence in God?

6. How does God guarantee to supply our needs as promised in Philippians 4:19?

7. How can you personally claim Philippians 4:19 in your own life?

8. Where are you placing your confidence today? What steps can you take to ensure that your confidence is in God alone?

Memory Verse

2 Corinthians 8:2

2 *How that in a great trial of affliction the abundance of their joy and their deep poverty abounded unto the riches of their liberality.*

LESSON NINE

Striving with Generous Living

Key Verses

2 Corinthians 8:1–9

1 *Moreover, brethren, we do you to wit of the grace of God bestowed on the churches of Macedonia;*

2 *How that in a great trial of affliction the abundance of their joy and their deep poverty abounded unto the riches of their liberality.*

3 *For to their power, I bear record, yea, and beyond their power they were willing of themselves;*

4 *Praying us with much intreaty that we would receive the gift, and take upon us the fellowship of the ministering to the saints.*

5 *And this they did, not as we hoped, but first gave their own selves to the Lord, and unto us by the will of God.*

6 *Insomuch that we desired Titus, that as he had begun, so he would also finish in you the same grace also.*

7 *Therefore, as ye abound in every thing, in faith, and utterance, and knowledge, and in all diligence, and in your love to us, see that ye abound in this grace also.*

8 *I speak not by commandment, but by occasion of the forwardness of others, and to prove the sincerity of your love.*

9 *For ye know the grace of our Lord Jesus Christ, that, though he was rich, yet for your sakes he became poor, that ye through his poverty might be rich.*

Overview

In his second letter to the Corinthians, Paul challenged them to strive together in a special offering that would be received in the near future. We can learn from his instructions, in preparation for giving to God through our local church.

Introduction

____

____

____

1 CORINTHIANS 9:5
5 Therefore I thought it necessary to exhort the brethren, that they would go before unto you, and make up beforehand your bounty, whereof ye had notice before, that the same might be ready, as a matter of bounty, and not as of covetousness.

I. The ______________________ of Generous Living (8:1–4)

A. They ________________ God's grace. (v. 1)

1 CORINTHIANS 15:10
10 But by the grace of God I am what I am: and his grace which was bestowed upon me was not in vain; but I laboured more abundantly than they all: yet not I, but the grace of God which was with me.

B. They ________________ over difficulty. (v. 2)

1 CORINTHIANS 16:2
2 Upon the first day of the week **let every one of you** *lay by him in store, as God hath prospered him, that there be no gatherings when I come.*

C. They ______________________ their ability. (v. 3)

LUKE 1:37
37 *For with God nothing shall be impossible.*

Faith giving is trusting God to give through me what He would not otherwise give to me.—AUTHOR UNKNOWN

D. They ______________________ gave. (vv. 3–4)

2 CORINTHIANS 9:7
7 *Every man according as he purposeth in his heart, so let him give; not grudgingly, or of necessity: for God loveth a cheerful giver.*

II. The ____________________________ for Generous Living (8:5–9)

A. They _________________________ their hearts. (v. 5)

EXODUS 35:29
29 *The children of Israel brought a willing offering unto the LORD, every man and woman, whose heart made them willing to bring for all manner of work, which the LORD had commanded to be made by the hand of Moses.*

B. They ____________________ spiritually. (v. 7)

MALACHI 3:10
10 *Bring ye all the tithes into the storehouse, that there may be meat in mine house, and prove me now herewith,*

saith the L*ORD* *of hosts, if I will not open you the windows of heaven, and pour you out a blessing, that there shall not be room enough to receive it.*

PROVERBS 3:9
9 *Honour the* L*ORD* *with thy substance, and with the firstfruits of all thine increase:*

C. They ________________ sincerely. (v. 8)

2 CORINTHIANS 8:24
24 *Wherefore shew ye to them, and before the churches, the proof of your love, and of our boasting on your behalf.*

1 JOHN 3:18
18 *My little children, let us not love in word, neither in tongue; but in deed and in truth.*

D. They ___________________ their Saviour's example. (v. 9)

MARK 10:45
45 *For even the Son of man came not to be ministered unto, but to minister, and to give his life a ransom for many.*

III. The ______________________ of Generous Living (8:12–9:11)

A. There was an ____________________ ____________________. (v. 12)

2 Corinthians 8:12
12 *For if there be first a willing mind, it is accepted according to that a man hath, and not according to that he hath not.*

Exodus 4:2
2 *And the Lord said unto him, What is that in thine hand? And he said, A rod.*

Exodus 3:22
22 *But every woman shall borrow of her neighbour, and of her that sojourneth in her house, jewels of silver, and jewels of gold, and raiment: and ye shall put them upon your sons, and upon your daughters; and ye shall spoil the Egyptians.*

John 2:6
6 *And there were set there six waterpots of stone, after the manner of the purifying of the Jews, containing two or three firkins apiece.*

John 6:9
9 *There is a lad here, which hath five barley loaves, and two small fishes: but what are they among so many?*

B. There was an ____________________ ____________________________. (vv. 13–15)

2 Corinthians 8:13–15
13 *For I mean not that other men be eased, and ye burdened:*
14 *But by an equality, that now at this time your abundance may be a supply for their want, that their abundance also may be a supply for your want: that there may be equality:*

15 As it is written, He that had gathered much had nothing over; and he that had gathered little had no lack.

C. There was an __________________ ________________________. (9:3–7)

2 CORINTHIANS 9:3–7

3 Yet have I sent the brethren, lest our boasting of you should be in vain in this behalf; that, as I said, ye may be ready:

4 Lest haply if they of Macedonia come with me, and find you unprepared, we (that we say not, ye) should be ashamed in this same confident boasting.

5 Therefore I thought it necessary to exhort the brethren, that they would go before unto you, and make up beforehand your bounty, whereof ye had notice before, that the same might be ready, as a matter of bounty, and not as of covetousness.

6 But this I say, He which soweth sparingly shall reap also sparingly; and he which soweth bountifully shall reap also bountifully.

7 Every man according as he purposeth in his heart, so let him give; not grudgingly, or of necessity: for God loveth a cheerful giver.

D. There was an ________________________ __________________________________. (9:8–11)

2 CORINTHIANS 9:8–11

8 And God is able to make all grace abound toward you; that ye, always having all sufficiency in all things, may abound to every good work:

9 (As it is written, He hath dispersed abroad; he hath given to the poor: his righteousness remaineth for ever.
10 Now he that ministereth seed to the sower both minister bread for your food, and multiply your seed sown, and increase the fruits of your righteousness;)
11 Being enriched in every thing to all bountifulness, which causeth through us thanksgiving to God.

Psalm 37:25
25 I have been young, and now am old; yet have I not seen the righteous forsaken, nor his seed begging bread.

Conclusion

____

____

____

Study Questions

1. Describe the financial state of the Macedonian believers according to 2 Corinthians 8:2.

2. In verse 3 of our text, what words describe the extent of the believers' willingness to give?

3. In verse 5, what did the Macedonians give first?

4. Write out 1 John 3:18 and describe how this command applies to giving.

5. When it comes to generous living, Who is our greatest example and what did He give?

6. What has God taught you recently about tithing, either from His Word or through personal experience as He demonstrated His faithfulness?

7. Second Corinthians 9:3–6 teaches us to prepare to live generously. What personal adjustments can you make as you strive to give generously to the Lord?

8. What promise is found in Psalm 37:25?

Memory Verse

Psalm 37:25
25 I have been young, and now am old; yet have I not seen the righteous forsaken, nor his seed begging bread.

LESSON TEN

Striving toward Maturity

Key Verses

EPHESIANS 4:11–16

11 *And he gave some, apostles; and some, prophets; and some, evangelists; and some, pastors and teachers;*

12 *For the perfecting of the saints, for the work of the ministry, for the edifying of the body of Christ:*

13 *Till we all come in the unity of the faith, and of the knowledge of the Son of God, unto a perfect man, unto the measure of the stature of the fulness of Christ:*

14 *That we henceforth be no more children, tossed to and fro, and carried about with every wind of doctrine, by the sleight of men, and cunning craftiness, whereby they lie in wait to deceive;*

15 *But speaking the truth in love, may grow up into him in all things, which is the head, even Christ:*

16 *From whom the whole body fitly joined together and compacted by that which every joint supplieth, according to the effectual working in the measure of every part, maketh increase of the body unto the edifying of itself in love.*

Overview

We must work together, assisting one another to become like Christ, as we strive toward maturity. Spiritual growth and forward progress are not optional, and we are responsible to one another for success in these areas.

Introduction

____

____

____

I. The ____________________ toward Maturity (vv. 7–12)

A. We have been given spiritual __________. (v. 7)

Ephesians 4:7
7 But unto every one of us is given grace according to the measure of the gift of Christ.

2 Corinthians 8:7
7 Therefore, as ye abound in every thing, in faith, and utterance, and knowledge, and in all diligence, and in your love to us, see that ye abound in this grace also.

2 Peter 3:18
18 But grow in grace, and in the knowledge of our Lord and Saviour Jesus Christ. To him be glory both now and for ever. Amen.

B. We have been given spiritual __________. (vv. 8–11)

Colossians 4:12–13
12 Epaphras, who is one of you, a servant of Christ, saluteth you, always labouring fervently for you in prayers,

that ye may stand perfect and complete in all the will of God.
13 *For I bear him record, that he hath a great zeal for you, and them that are in Laodicea, and them in Hierapolis.*

C. *We have been given a spiritual ________. (v. 12)*

1 Peter 4:10
10 *As every man hath received the gift, even so minister the same one to another, as good stewards of the manifold grace of God.*

II. The ________________ of Maturity (v. 13)

2 Corinthians 10:12
12 *For we dare not make ourselves of the number, or compare ourselves with some that commend themselves: but they measuring themselves by themselves, and comparing themselves among themselves, are not wise.*

A. *There should be ______________ with the ________________. (v. 13a)*

Philippians 1:27
27 *Only let your conversation be as it becometh the gospel of Christ: that whether I come and see you, or else be absent, I may hear of your affairs, that ye stand fast in one spirit, with one mind striving together for the faith of the gospel;*

B. There should be ________________________ to the ________________________. (v. 13b)

ROMANS 8:29

29 For whom he did foreknow, he also did predestinate to be conformed to the image of his Son, that he might be the firstborn among many brethren.

ROMANS 12:1

1 I beseech you therefore, brethren, by the mercies of God, that ye present your bodies a living sacrifice, holy, acceptable unto God, which is your reasonable service.

III. The ________________ of Maturity (vv. 14–16)

A. There are three telling marks of ________________________. (v. 14)

1. Unstable in ________________

JAMES 1:8

8 A double minded man is unstable in all his ways.

2. Unsure of ________________

3. Unable to ________________

HEBREWS 5:14

14 But strong meat belongeth to them that are of full age, even those who by reason of use have their senses exercised to discern both good and evil.

COLOSSIANS 2:6–8

6 As ye have therefore received Christ Jesus the Lord, so walk ye in him:

7 Rooted and built up in him, and stablished in the faith, as ye have been taught, abounding therein with thanksgiving.

8 Beware lest any man spoil you through philosophy and vain deceit, after the tradition of men, after the rudiments of the world, and not after Christ.

B. *There are three triumphant marks of ______________________________. (vv. 15–16)*

1. ______________________________ that's meaningful

COLOSSIANS 4:6

6 Let your speech be alway with grace, seasoned with salt, that ye may know how ye ought to answer every man.

2. A ______________________________ mindset

COLOSSIANS 1:18

18 And he is the head of the body, the church: who is the beginning, the firstborn from the dead; that in all things he might have the preeminence.

3. A ______________________ to the members

1 CORINTHIANS 12:21–22

21 And the eye cannot say unto the hand, I have no need of thee: nor again the head to the feet, I have no need of you.

22 Nay, much more those members of the body, which seem to be more feeble, are necessary:

Conclusion

Study Questions

1. According to Ephesians 4:11, what gift did God give to the Philippian believers to help in their spiritual maturity?

2. What spiritual goals are accomplished through the body of Christ as a result of the influence of its spiritual leaders (Ephesians 4:12)?

3. In what two ways can we measure our maturity?

4. What is one sign of spiritual immaturity?

5. What is one indicator of spiritual maturity?

6. According to Ephesians 4:15, how should we speak?

7. How would you describe your level of devotion to Christ and His church? What areas need improvement?

8. What is one thing you can do to edify other members of Christ's body this week?

Memory Verses

Colossians 2:6–7

6 *As ye have therefore received Christ Jesus the Lord, so walk ye in him:*

7 *Rooted and built up in him, and stablished in the faith, as ye have been taught, abounding there in with thanksgiving.*

Striving as the Body of Christ

Key Verses

1 CORINTHIANS 12:12–14, 27

12 *For as the body is one, and hath many members, and all the members of that one body, being many, are one body: so also is Christ.*

13 *For by one Spirit are we all baptized into one body, whether we be Jews or Gentiles, whether we be bond or free; and have been all made to drink into one Spirit.*

14 *For the body is not one member, but many.*

27 *Now ye are the body of Christ, and members in particular.*

Overview

The concept of striving together as a local church is illustrated no better than by the biblical metaphor of the body of Christ. When we consider the local church as a body, we will appreciate the variety among our members and accept our responsibility to one another.

Introduction

____

____

____

Romans 12:4–5

4 *For as we have many members in one body, and all members have not the same office:*

5 *So we, being many, are one body in Christ, and every one members one of another.*

Ephesians 1:23

23 *Which is his body, the fulness of him that filleth all in all.*

Ephesians 4:12

12 *For the perfecting of the saints, for the work of the ministry, for the edifying of the body of Christ:*

Colossians 1:24

24 *Who now rejoice in my sufferings for you, and fill up that which is behind of the afflictions of Christ in my flesh for his body's sake, which is the church:*

Colossians 2:19

19 *And not holding the Head, from which all the body by joints and bands having nourishment ministered, and knit together, increaseth with the increase of God.*

I. The ________________ of the ___________ (vv. 4–11)

ACTS 1:4

4 And, being assembled together with them, commanded them that they should not depart from Jerusalem, but wait for the promise of the Father, which, saith he, ye have heard of me.

A. He provides the miracle of _____________. (vv. 4–7)

1 CORINTHIANS 12:4–7

4 Now there are diversities of gifts, but the same Spirit.

5 And there are differences of administrations, but the same Lord.

6 And there are diversities of operations, but it is the same God which worketh all in all.

7 But the manifestation of the Spirit is given to every man to profit withal.

B. He provides a mosaic of _______________. (vv. 8–11)

1 CORINTHIANS 12:8–11

8 For to one is given by the Spirit the word of wisdom; to another the word of knowledge by the same Spirit;

9 To another faith by the same Spirit; to another the gifts of healing by the same Spirit;

10 To another the working of miracles; to another prophecy; to another discerning of spirits; to another divers kinds of tongues; to another the interpretation of tongues:

11 But all these worketh that one and the selfsame Spirit, dividing to every man severally as he will.

Romans 12:6–8

6 Having then gifts differing according to the grace that is given to us, whether prophecy, let us prophesy according to the proportion of faith;
7 Or ministry, let us wait on our ministering: or he that teacheth, on teaching;
8 Or he that exhorteth, on exhortation: he that giveth, let him do it with simplicity; he that ruleth, with diligence; he that sheweth mercy, with cheerfulness.

1 Corinthians 12:11

11 But all these worketh that one and the selfsame Spirit, dividing to every man severally as he will.

Romans 9:20

20 Nay but, O man, who art thou that repliest against God? Shall the thing formed say to him that formed it, Why hast thou made me thus?

II. The ____________________ of the ____________ (vv. 12–21)

Acts 20:29

29 For I know this, that after my departing shall grievous wolves enter in among you, not sparing the flock.

Luke 12:32

32 Fear not, little flock; for it is your Father's good pleasure to give you the kingdom.

1 Corinthians 3:19

19 For the wisdom of this world is foolishness with God. For it is written, He taketh the wise in their own craftiness.

Ephesians 2:21

21 In whom all the building fitly framed together groweth unto an holy temple in the Lord:

1 Peter 4:17

17 For the time is come that judgment must begin at the house of God: and if it first begin at us, what shall the end be of them that obey not the gospel of God?

1 Peter 2:5

5 Ye also, as lively stones, are built up a spiritual house, an holy priesthood, to offer up spiritual sacrifices, acceptable to God by Jesus Christ.

1 Timothy 3:15

15 But if I tarry long, that thou mayest know how thou oughtest to behave thyself in the house of God, which is the church of the living God, the pillar and ground of the truth.

2 Corinthians 11:2

2 For I am jealous over you with godly jealousy: for I have espoused you to one husband, that I may present you as a chaste virgin to Christ.

Revelation 19:7

7 Let us be glad and rejoice, and give honour to him: for the marriage of the Lamb is come, and his wife hath made herself ready.

A. We are ____________ and yet we are ________ body. (vv. 12–14)

1 Corinthians 12:12–14

12 *For as the body is one, and hath many members, and all the members of that one body, being many, are one body: so also is Christ.*
13 *For by one Spirit are we all baptized into one body, whether we be Jews or Gentiles, whether we be bond or free; and have been all made to drink into one Spirit.*
14 *For the body is not one member, but many.*

John 17:20–22

20 *Neither pray I for these alone, but for them also which shall believe on me through their word;*
21 *That they all may be one; as thou, Father, art in me, and I in thee, that they also may be one in us: that the world may believe that thou hast sent me.*
22 *And the glory which thou gavest me I have given them; that they may be one, even as we are one:*

B. We are ____________________ when we ____________________ within the body. (vv. 15–16)

1 Corinthians 12:15–16

15 *If the foot shall say, Because I am not the hand, I am not of the body; is it therefore not of the body?*
16 *And if the ear shall say, Because I am not the eye, I am not of the body; is it therefore not of the body?*

2 Corinthians 10:12

12 *For we dare not make ourselves of the number, or compare ourselves with some that commend themselves:*

but they measuring themselves by themselves, and comparing themselves among themselves, are not wise.

C. *We are __________ purposefully __________ for the body. (vv. 17–20)*

1 CORINTHIANS 12:17–20

17 *If the whole body were an eye, where were the hearing? If the whole were hearing, where were the smelling?*
18 *But now hath God set the members every one of them in the body, as it hath pleased him.*
19 *And if they were all one member, where were the body?*
20 *But now are they many members, yet but one body.*

1 PETER 4:10

10 *As every man hath received the gift, even so minister the same one to another, as good stewards of the manifold grace of God.*

D. *We are __________ for __________________ within the body. (v. 21)*

1 CORINTHIANS 12:21

21 *And the eye cannot say unto the hand, I have no need of thee: nor again the head to the feet, I have no need of you.*

ROMANS 14:7

7 *For none of us liveth to himself, and no man dieth to himself.*

GALATIANS 6:2

2 *Bear ye one another's burdens, and so fulfil the law of Christ.*

III. The ________________ of the ________________ (vv. 22–31)

ROMANS 12:4–5

4 *For as we have many members in one body, and all members have not the same office:*

5 *So we, being many, are one body in Christ, and every one members one of another.*

A. There is a ____________ about the members. (vv. 22–24)

1 CORINTHIANS 12:22–24

22 *Nay, much more those members of the body, which seem to be more feeble, are necessary:*

23 *And those members of the body, which we think to be less honourable, upon these we bestow more abundant honour; and our uncomely parts have more abundant comeliness.*

24 *For our comely parts have no need: but God hath tempered the body together, having given more abundant honour to that part which lacked:*

1 CORINTHIANS 1:26–29

26 *For ye see your calling, brethren, how that not many wise men after the flesh, not many mighty, not many noble, are called:*

27 *But God hath chosen the foolish things of the world to confound the wise; and God hath chosen the weak things of the world to confound the things which are mighty;*

28 *And base things of the world, and things which are despised, hath God chosen, yea, and things which are not, to bring to nought things that are:*

29 *That no flesh should glory in his presence.*

B. There is a ________________ among the members. (vv. 25–26)

1 CORINTHIANS 12:25–26

25 *That there should be no schism in the body; but that the members should have the same care one for another.*
26 *And whether one member suffer, all the members suffer with it; or one member be honoured, all the members rejoice with it.*

EPHESIANS 4:12, 16

12 *For the perfecting of the saints, for the work of the ministry, for the edifying of the body of Christ:*
16 *From whom the whole body fitly joined together and compacted by that which every joint supplieth, according to the effectual working in the measure of every part, maketh increase of the body unto the edifying of itself in love.*

C. There is a ________________ above the members. (v. 27)

1 CORINTHIANS 12:27

27 *Now ye are the body of Christ, and members in particular.*

EPHESIANS 1:22–23

22 *And hath put all things under his feet, and gave him to be the head over all things to the church,*
23 *Which is his body, the fulness of him that filleth all in all.*

EPHESIANS 5:23

23 *For the husband is the head of the wife, even as Christ is the head of the church: and he is the saviour of the body.*

D. There is a ____________________ available to the members. (vv. 28–31)

1 Corinthians 12:28–31

28 *And God hath set some in the church, first apostles, secondarily prophets, thirdly teachers, after that miracles, then gifts of healings, helps, governments, diversities of tongues.*

29 *Are all apostles? are all prophets? are all teachers? are all workers of miracles?*

30 *Have all the gifts of healing? do all speak with tongues? do all interpret?*

31 *But covet earnestly the best gifts: and yet shew I unto you a more excellent way.*

Conclusion

____

____

____

Study Questions

1. What two things does the Holy Spirit provide in the context of the body of Christ?

2. What is the purpose of spiritual gifts?

3. According to 1 Corinthians 12:15–16, what are we to avoid within the body of Christ?

4. What does 1 Corinthians 12:21 tell us about our relationships with other members of the body of Christ?

5. Write out Galatians 6:2.

6. Who is the Head of the body?

7. What are your spiritual gifts?* How can you exercise your gifts as you minister with other members of the body?

8. How can you promote a spirit of unity and edification among the members of the body of Christ?

Memory Verses

Romans 12:4–5

4 For as we have many members in one body, and all members have not the same office:

5 So we, being many, are one body in Christ, and every one members one of another.

---

*If you are unsure of what your spiritual gifts are, download a free copy of "The Spiritual Gifts Test" from strivingtogether.com.

LESSON TWELVE

Striving through Difficulty

Key Verses

ACTS 16:16–25

16 And it came to pass, as we went to prayer, a certain damsel possessed with a spirit of divination met us, which brought her masters much gain by soothsaying:

17 The same followed Paul and us, and cried, saying, These men are the servants of the most high God, which shew unto us the way of salvation.

18 And this did she many days. But Paul, being grieved, turned and said to the spirit, I command thee in the name of Jesus Christ to come out of her. And he came out the same hour.

19 And when her masters saw that the hope of their gains was gone, they caught Paul and Silas, and drew them into the marketplace unto the rulers,

20 And brought them to the magistrates, saying, These men, being Jews, do exceedingly trouble our city,

21 And teach customs, which are not lawful for us to receive, neither to observe, being Romans.

22 And the multitude rose up together against them: and the magistrates rent off their clothes, and commanded to beat them.

23 And when they had laid many stripes upon them, they cast them into prison, charging the jailor to keep them safely:

24 Who, having received such a charge, thrust them into the inner prison, and made their feet fast in the stocks.

25 And at midnight Paul and Silas prayed, and sang praises unto God: and the prisoners heard them.

Overview

Every Christian will encounter difficulty. In the midst of difficulty we have been called to both draw strength from other believers and to offer strength to our fellow believers. If there were ever a time to strive together, it is when we encounter difficult circumstances.

Introduction

____

____

____

John 16:33

33 These things I have spoken unto you, that in me ye might have peace. In the world ye shall have tribulation: but be of good cheer; I have overcome the world.

Your response is your responsibility.—Emerson Eggerichs

1 Peter 4:16, 19

16 Yet if any man suffer as a Christian, let him not be ashamed; but let him glorify God on this behalf.
19 Wherefore let them that suffer according to the will of God commit the keeping of their souls to him in well doing, as unto a faithful Creator.

I. The ______________ they Encountered

Acts 16:9–19

9 And a vision appeared to Paul in the night; There stood a man of Macedonia, and prayed him, saying, Come over into Macedonia, and help us.
10 And after he had seen the vision, immediately we endeavoured to go into Macedonia, assuredly gathering that the Lord had called us for to preach the gospel unto them.
11 Therefore loosing from Troas, we came with a straight course to Samothracia, and the next day to Neapolis;

12 And from thence to Philippi, which is the chief city of that part of Macedonia, and a colony: and we were in that city abiding certain days.
13 And on the sabbath we went out of the city by a river side, where prayer was wont to be made; and we sat down, and spake unto the women which resorted thither.
14 And a certain woman named Lydia, a seller of purple, of the city of Thyatira, which worshipped God, heard us: whose heart the Lord opened, that she attended unto the things which were spoken of Paul.
15 And when she was baptized, and her household, she besought us, saying, If ye have judged me to be faithful to the Lord, come into my house, and abide there. And she constrained us.
16 And it came to pass, as we went to prayer, a certain damsel possessed with a spirit of divination met us, which brought her masters much gain by soothsaying:
17 The same followed Paul and us, and cried, saying, These men are the servants of the most high God, which shew unto us the way of salvation.
18 And this did she many days. But Paul, being grieved, turned and said to the spirit, I command thee in the name of Jesus Christ to come out of her. And he came out the same hour.
19 And when her masters saw that the hope of their gains was gone, they caught Paul and Silas, and drew them into the marketplace unto the rulers,

A. *They were living out God's ________________. (vv. 9–10)*

B. *They were living for God's ________________. (vv. 16–18)*

Philippians 3:13–14
13 *Brethren, I count not myself to have apprehended: but this one thing I do, forgetting those things which are behind, and reaching forth unto those things which are before,*
14 *I press toward the mark for the prize of the high calling of God in Christ Jesus.*

C. *They were living under God's ____________________. (v. 19)*

Job 23:10
10 *But he knoweth the way that I take: when he hath tried me, I shall come forth as gold.*

II. The ______________ they Endured

Acts 16:20–25
20 *And brought them to the magistrates, saying, These men, being Jews, do exceedingly trouble our city,*
21 *And teach customs, which are not lawful for us to receive, neither to observe, being Romans.*
22 *And the multitude rose up together against them: and the magistrates rent off their clothes, and commanded to beat them.*
23 *And when they had laid many stripes upon them, they cast them into prison, charging the jailor to keep them safely:*
24 *Who, having received such a charge, thrust them into the inner prison, and made their feet fast in the stocks.*
25 *And at midnight Paul and Silas prayed, and sang praises unto God: and the prisoners heard them.*

A. They endured ______________________________
______________________________. (vv. 20–21)

MATTHEW 5:11
11 *Blessed are ye, when men shall revile you, and persecute you, and shall say all manner of evil against you falsely, for my sake.*

B. They endured ______________________________
______________________________. (v. 22)

2 TIMOTHY 3:12
12 *Yea, and all that will live godly in Christ Jesus shall suffer persecution.*

C. They endured ______________________________
______________________________. (v. 23)

JOHN 15:20
20 *Remember the word that I said unto you, the servant is not greater than his lord. If they have persecuted me, they will also persecute you; if they have kept my saying, they will keep yours also.*

D. They endured ______________________________
______________________________. (v. 24)

2 CORINTHIANS 11:23–27
23 *Are they ministers of Christ? (I speak as a fool) I am more; in labours more abundant, in stripes above measure, in prisons more frequent, in deaths oft.*
24 *Of the Jews five times received I forty stripes save one.*

25 Thrice was I beaten with rods, once was I stoned, thrice I suffered shipwreck, a night and a day I have been in the deep;
26 In journeyings often, in perils of waters, in perils of robbers, in perils by mine own countrymen, in perils by the heathen, in perils in the city, in perils in the wilderness, in perils in the sea, in perils among false brethren;
27 In weariness and painfulness, in watchings often, in hunger and thirst, in fastings often, in cold and nakedness.

III. The ______________ they Experienced

A. The prisoners were ____________________. (vv. 25–26)

Acts 16:25–26
25 And at midnight Paul and Silas prayed, and sang praises unto God: and the prisoners heard them.
26 And suddenly there was a great earthquake, so that the foundations of the prison were shaken: and immediately all the doors were opened, and every one's bands were loosed.

B. The jailor was ________________. (vv. 27–34)

Acts 16:27–34
27 And the keeper of the prison awaking out of his sleep, and seeing the prison doors open, he drew out his sword, and would have killed himself, supposing that the prisoners had been fled.
28 But Paul cried with a loud voice, saying, Do thyself no harm: for we are all here.

29 Then he called for a light, and sprang in, and came trembling, and fell down before Paul and Silas,
30 And brought them out, and said, Sirs, what must I do to be saved?
31 And they said, Believe on the Lord Jesus Christ, and thou shalt be saved, and thy house.
32 And they spake unto him the word of the Lord, and to all that were in his house.
33 And he took them the same hour of the night, and washed their stripes; and was baptized, he and all his, straightway.
34 And when he had brought them into his house, he set meat before them, and rejoiced, believing in God with all his house.

2 CORINTHIANS 5:17
17 If any man be in Christ, he is a new creature: old things are passed away; behold, all things are become new.

C. The city was ________________. (vv. 35–39)

ACTS 16:35–39
35 And when it was day, the magistrates sent the serjeants, saying, Let those men go.
36 And the keeper of the prison told this saying to Paul, The magistrates have sent to let you go: now therefore depart, and go in peace.
37 But Paul said unto them, They have beaten us openly uncondemned, being Romans, and have cast us into prison; and now do they thrust us out privily? nay verily; but let them come themselves and fetch us out.
38 And the serjeants told these words unto the magistrates: and they feared, when they heard that they were Romans.

39 And they came and besought them, and brought them out, and desired them to depart out of the city.

D. The believers were ______________. *(v. 40)*

ACTS 16:40

40 And they went out of the prison, and entered into the house of Lydia: and when they had seen the brethren, they comforted them, and departed.

2 CORINTHIANS 1:3–4

3 Blessed be God, even the Father of our Lord Jesus Christ, the Father of mercies, and the God of all comfort;
4 Who comforteth us in all our tribulation, that we may be able to comfort them which are in any trouble, by the comfort wherewith we ourselves are comforted of God.

Conclusion

____

____

____

Study Questions

1. Who was Paul's faithful friend, striving together with him during their difficulties?

2. Write out 2 Timothy 3:12.

3. What miracle did God perform in the middle of Paul and Silas' difficult time?

4. Are you currently living out God's specific plan for your life? If not, what specific steps can you take to ensure that you are in the center of God's will?

5. How can the truth of God's providence comfort you during times of difficulty?

6. Others were saved as a result of Paul and Silas striving together. Who can you partner with to systematically (perhaps through your church outreach programs) tell others about the gospel?

7. Like Paul and Silas, we all have "bad days"—days when everything seems to go wrong. What can we do in response to these frustrating experiences?

8. God has given us the comfort of other believers to help during times of trial and difficulty. Who can you be a blessing to this week?

Memory Verse

Job 23:10

10 But he knoweth the way that I take: when he hath tried me, I shall come forth as gold.

LESSON THIRTEEN

Striving to Reach Souls

Key Verses

ACTS 8:1–8

1 *And Saul was consenting unto his death. And at that time there was a great persecution against the church which was at Jerusalem; and they were all scattered abroad throughout the regions of Judaea and Samaria, except the apostles.*

2 *And devout men carried Stephen to his burial, and made great lamentation over him.*

3 *As for Saul, he made havock of the church, entering into every house, and haling men and women committed them to prison.*

4 *Therefore they that were scattered abroad went every where preaching the word.*

5 *Then Philip went down to the city of Samaria, and preached Christ unto them.*

6 *And the people with one accord gave heed unto those things which Philip spake, hearing and seeing the miracles which he did.*

7 *For unclean spirits, crying with loud voice, came out of many that were possessed with them: and many taken with palsies, and that were lame, were healed.*

8 *And there was great joy in that city.*

Overview

There was a passion to lead others to Christ within the hearts of the first century Christians. This passion propelled them to courageously share the gospel of Christ, even in the face of fierce persecution. We must duplicate this passion today if we are to fulfill the call of God on our lives and church.

Introduction

____

____

____

I. The Scattering of the ______________ (vv. 1–8)

A. They were scattered by severe ________________________. (vv. 1–3)

James 1:1–3

1 *James, a servant of God and of the Lord Jesus Christ, to the twelve tribes which are scattered abroad, greeting.*

2 *My brethren, count it all joy when ye fall into divers temptations;*

3 *Knowing this, that the trying of your faith worketh patience.*

B. They were scattered but still ________________________. (vv. 4–8, 25)

Acts 8:25

25 *And they, when they had testified and preached the word of the Lord, returned to Jerusalem, and preached the gospel in many villages of the Samaritans.*

Genesis 50:20

20 But as for you, ye thought evil against me; but God meant it unto good, to bring to pass, as it is this day, to save much people alive.

Romans 8:28

28 And we know that all things work together for good to them that love God, to them who are the called according to his purpose.

The test of your character is what it takes to stop you. —Dr. Bob Jones, Sr.

2 Corinthians 4:8–11

8 We are troubled on every side, yet not distressed; we are perplexed, but not in despair;

9 Persecuted, but not forsaken; cast down, but not destroyed;

10 Always bearing about in the body the dying of the Lord Jesus, that the life also of Jesus might be made manifest in our body.

11 For we which live are alway delivered unto death for Jesus' sake, that the life also of Jesus might be made manifest in our mortal flesh.

II. The Spirit of the ________________ (vv. 26–31)

A. We must have a spirit of ______________. (vv. 26–28)

The only alternative to soulwinning is disobedience to Christ.—Curtis Hutson

Acts 8:26–28

26 And the angel of the Lord spake unto Philip, saying, Arise, and go toward the south unto the way that goeth down from Jerusalem unto Gaza, which is desert.

27 And he arose and went: and, behold, a man of Ethiopia, an eunuch of great authority under Candace queen of the Ethiopians, who had the charge of all her treasure, and had come to Jerusalem for to worship,

28 Was returning, and sitting in his chariot read Esaias the prophet.

Proverbs 37:23

23 The steps of a good man are ordered by the Lord: and he delighteth in his way.

B. *We must have a spirit of ____________________. (v. 30a)*

Acts 8:30

30 And Philip ran thither to him...

John 9:4

4 I must work the works of him that sent me, while it is day: the night cometh, when no man can work.

C. *We must have a spirit of ____________________. (v. 30–31)*

Acts 8:30–31

30 And Philip ran thither to him, and heard him read the prophet Esaias, and said, Understandest thou what thou readest?

31 And he said, How can I, except some man should guide me? And he desired Philip that he would come up and sit with him.

MATTHEW 28:18
18 And we know that all things work together for good to them that love God, to them who are the called according to his purpose.

PROVERBS 28:1
1 The wicked flee when no man pursueth: but the righteous are bold as a lion.

III. The Salvation of a ____________ (vv. 32–39)

A. The significance of the ________________ must be understood. (vv. 32–33)

ACTS 8:32–33
32 The place of the scripture which he read was this, He was led as a sheep to the slaughter; and like a lamb dumb before his shearer, so opened he not his mouth:
33 In his humiliation his judgment was taken away: and who shall declare his generation? for his life is taken from the earth.

GALATIANS 3:24
24 Wherefore the law was our schoolmaster to bring us unto Christ, that we might be justified by faith.

Romans 7:7
7 What shall we say then? Is the law sin? God forbid. Nay, I had not known sin, but by the law: for I had not known lust, except the law had said, Thou shalt not covet.

Isaiah 55:11
11 So shall my word be that goeth forth out of my mouth: it shall not return unto me void, but it shall accomplish that which I please, and it shall prosper in the thing whereto I sent it.

Romans 10:17
17 So then faith cometh by hearing, and hearing by the word of God.

B. *The sacrifice of the ________________ must be proclaimed. (vv. 34–35)*

Acts 8:34–35
34 And the eunuch answered Philip, and said, I pray thee, of whom speaketh the prophet this? of himself, or of some other man?
35 Then Philip opened his mouth, and began at the same scripture, and preached unto him Jesus.

Isaiah 53:5–6
5 But he was wounded for our transgressions, he was bruised for our iniquities: the chastisement of our peace was upon him; and with his stripes we are healed.
6 All we like sheep have gone astray; we have turned every one to his own way; and the Lord hath laid on him the iniquity of us all.

C. The step of ______________________ must be taken. (vv. 36–39)

ACTS 8:36–39

36 And as they went on their way, they came unto a certain water: and the eunuch said, See, here is water; what doth hinder me to be baptized?

37 And Philip said, If thou believest with all thine heart, thou mayest. And he answered and said, I believe that Jesus Christ is the Son of God.

38 And he commanded the chariot to stand still: and they went down both into the water, both Philip and the eunuch; and he baptized him.

39 And when they were come up out of the water, the Spirit of the Lord caught away Philip, that the eunuch saw him no more: and he went on his way rejoicing.

ROMANS 6:4

4 Therefore we are buried with him by baptism into death: that like as Christ was raised up from the dead by the glory of the Father, even so we also should walk in newness of life.

Conclusion

____

____

____

Study Questions

1. What caused the saints to scatter?

2. What three qualities should describe our spirit in soulwinning?

3. Who demonstrated great boldness in Acts 8:31?

4. Who did Philip witness to?

5. When it comes to sharing our faith, it is often easier to offer excuses than it is to take opportunities. What excuses do you find yourself offering most frequently? What hinders you from seizing God-ordained opportunities to share your faith?